The Dark Side of My Mind

Volume 7

Briana Blair

The Dark Side of My Mind Volume 7

ISBN 978-0-557-76136-4

Contact me: webmaster@bluedragoncreations.com

Visit my website: http://bluedragoncreations.com/gallery/

Table of Contents

Volume 7

Poems 241 - 280

River - July 1997

Shut out

Closed off

Dammed up

Like so much unwanted water

From the river

But like that river

I will burst that dam

And flood upon their banks

And wash them all away

With my current

Take You Down - July 1997

The end is here

My time has come

But I am not the only one

For I will take you down

Yes, I will take you with me

You'll wallow in the mud and shit

And crawl around this filthy pit

'Cause I will take you down

To the darkened corners of this cell

And down into the depths of hell

Yes

I will take you with me

When I die

Remember Me - July 1997

When the world comes down

Comes crashing down around our ears

Like so much rubble

Remember me

Remember how I loved like no other

How through my heartache and pain

I remained

How through my tears I found you

And held you as we fell

Remember me

When all the world is black

And we are all alone

Reach out to me

Place me at your heart

And let me smile

Sway - July 1997

Swaying

Swooping

Sliding back and forth

Like on an ocean

Murky mingling

Feelings meeting

Still swaying?

Maybe

Staggering like an alcoholic daze

Moving, but not

Feeling the waves

When you're standing still

With groggy, foggy

Sights ahead

Full of feeling

Empty of direction

Motion and way

Must meet

Then clarity is formed

Eaten - August 1997

It eats at me

Devouring me

From the inside out

It consumes my mind

And gorges on my soul

It feasts upon my despair

And sustains life from my hate

Each day I feel the gnawing

Of death's razor sharp teeth

And now so little is left to offer

For I have been eaten

The Holding - August 1997

The holding

Is heaven

With warm touch

And soft breath

Hair brushes my face

And arms embrace with love

Then a tender kiss

From warm lips

To warm lips

Still holding

And wishing

It could last forever

Daydreams - August 1997

Daydreams

Drifting lightly

Over unknown spaces

Wandering

Reaching out

To untouched places

Floating

Wishing

For better things

This

Is where

My heart sings

The Border - August 1997

The sun shines above

But there is darkness ahead

Storms are brewing in the distance

Thunder rolls beyond

There is a thin line

Between the sunshine and the darkness

And there I stand

The wind blowing through my hair

And the raindrops stinging my face

And I'm at home

Here

But on the border to there

In the calm

At the edge of the hurricane

This is the place to be

Promises - August 1997

Promises made

And promises broken

The words were said

And simply tokens

To pay me for the pain

I'll feel tomorrow

As I feel today

Promises made

And promises breaking

You can't believe

The toll they're taking

And I want things to be true

All I want

Is the real you

Promises made

And promises kept

I'll forget

The times I wept

And now that we are free

Love will be

As it should be

Rat - August 1997

I am a rat in a cage

Will you feed me?

Will you give me water?

Will you let the light shine in

Or will you shake this cage

To hear me squeal?

Will you touch me

To calm my fear?

Or will you snap me

Like the twig you think I am?

I am not sure.

But I know you control me

And it displeases me.

But I am your animal

And my life

Is in your hands.

Winter - August 1997

Winter rushes upon us

Like a slasher's blade

Piercing deeply

Causing weakness

With no warning

But the sound

Of wind whistling like cold steel

And it comes

Pricking at first

And slashing after

And the winter's snows

Will freeze the bones

And chill the hearts of all

Bringing misery and despair

And burying all dreams of warmth

And the happiness is gone

With the coming of the winter

This House - September 1997

This house

Is not a home

It's not even a house

It's the casket in which we will die

But it must think we're already dead

For it decays all around us

The roof no longer keeps the outside out

Windows cannot be closed against the wind

The floors are rotting and nothing works

But we must stay here

There are no options

The poor must die

And so we shall

In this coffin we call home

Dreamworld Vs. Reality* - *September 1997

Sleep

A painful straying

From the daylight world

Once a place for dreams

Is now a place to be spent

On love and being loved

Stealing minutes of laughter

From hours of sorrow and hopelessness

I wish never to sleep

But stay in daylight

To grasp at ever-fading

Pieces of reality

Leaving sleep gives time for pleasure

Yet without sleep pain is ever present

And I appall this war

Between darkness and light

Between the dreamworld

And reality

Liar's Mask - September 1997

Oh, you sweet, innocent thing

Your façade does not amuse me

Do you call me a fool?

Oh, my sweet, I am no fool.

I know your deceit and your destruction

Do you know what I would give

To tear you apart?

I would shred you with my slashing nails

Peel you open with my angry fingers

Tear your heart out with a steady hand

And eat you like a lion's prize.

Your smiling face will lay

A liar's mask upon the dirt

And your evil will be gone from us

And I will have the strength to go on.

My Impossible Dream - September 1997

Now I will walk with you, Now I will talk with you

Now I will lay here In love in your arms

Once I was all alone

Once I was on my own

Now I know

That you'll always be near

Now when I walk with you

Now when I talk with you

Now I'll feel

Like I'm always at home

Now when I'm in your arms

Now when I hear your charms

I will know

That it's not just a dream

I though you were unreachable

I thought it could never be

I thought you were untouchable

But now you're here by my side

I thought my life would be lonely

But now here you are with me

And now I don't have to

Reach out in the darkness

For now I have

My impossible dream

Little Drops Of Hate - October 1997

Hate

Little drops of hate

Drip down into a space

Upon the floor

My anger writhes

And slips down off me

Into the puddle on the floor

Caused by my hate

And my despair oozes out

And drops like reeking masses

To my feet

And it continues

And I'm up to my knees in it

Encased by this stinking reality

Bound to the place where I stand

And the little drops of hate

And the little drips of anger

And the little bits of despair

Will continue to come

Until the filth of life consumes me

And it will

Drip…Drip…Drip…

Slave To The Pigs* - *October 1997

With blood and sweat upon my skin

I shovel the shit of the masses before me

And they care not about my pain

I am a slave

The wallowing pigs make me follow behind

Forever moving and scraping the remains of the day

I am a slave to the pigs

And they care not for my despair

For the slaves are but more trash

To be shoved from the view of the rich and the powerful

And those seen shall be trampled into dust

But I will not be dust

For I am an animal

And with claws of hate

And fangs of loathing

I will slash apart those pigs

Feast upon their bleeding souls

And trample upon what's left

And be slave to the pigs

Nevermore

***Color Me** - October 1997*

I am a picture

A mass of empty lines

Will you color me?

Color me blue for my sadness

Color me red for my anger

Color me black for my pain

Color me green for my envy of life

Color me violet for my soul

Color me white for my tears

Color me like a rainbow

Color me with care

I Alone - October 1997

I am I

All alone

A singular soul

I alone must face the torment

I alone must live through the storm

I alone must fight the battles

I alone

Yes I

Alone

For no one knows my suffering

No one understands my pain

There are no hands to pull me up

There are no hearts to pull me through

For I

Am I alone

I Want You - October 1997

I want you

Can you feel it?

Can you smell it?

Do you even realize

The passions that I've trapped inside

The hunger that I push away

Keep hidden from the light of day

Do you know?

Would you tell me?

Would you want me

To touch

And to taste?

I want you

I would savor you

Like fine wine

I could love you

Because I want you

Virginia - ***November 1997***

She was not my friend

But I cared for her.

She was not my blood

But I loved her.

She was not my mother

She was better.

I, just a young stranger

Was taken into her heart.

When I cried

She came to comfort me.

In my time of need

I was not alone.

And now, in her time of need

She will not be alone.

I will hold her hand

As she held mine.

And I will love her

As she loved me.

My heart will be with her always

And I will never forget her.

Dedicated to the memory of

-- Virginia Margaret Chevery - 1929-1998 --

Light of Love - December 1997

Hope

Springs eternal

In the hearts of lovers

So many things

Seem possible

In the light of love

Two hands touch

In times of darkness

And new worlds can emerge

When two souls join

A power is gained

And any hardship can be conquered

Though shadows fall

And skies turn grey

Joined thoughts can make a path

And anything is possible

When shining

In the light of love

Consumed - December 1997

Little bits of life

Eaten away

Rotted

Sold

Or broken

Chewed up

Never to be had again

Memories

That can't be touched

Things

So hard to remember

Taken

Consumed

Devoured

Gone

The Moon - January 1998

I see the moon

Full and round

Shining down upon my misery

Glowing

In my salty tears

And it smiles

He's laughing at me

My pain is his joy

It makes him glow

'Cause he knows

There's plenty more where this came from

So the moon will shine above

And he gives me no love

He just hangs there

And shines

Everything - *February 1998*

In the time of dark

I am a light

In a place of pain

I am relief

In a moment of hunger

I am your bread

When parched by thirst

I am your wine

When you are bitter

I am your honey

Taste me

Savor my love

As it drips down on you

Rejoice in me

I pray to be

Your everything

And as one

We are all anyone could need

Vampire* - *February 1998

Gleaming teeth

In white night shine

Sharpened fangs

Piercing my mind

Hell is here

And I embrace it

Your blood is hot

And I can taste it

I am free

No one can stop me

I am death

No one can top me

I am vampire

Here to kill you

I am freedom

Here to thrill you

I will bite

And set you free

Come with me

And you will be

Vampire

Liquid Thought - February 1998

I've got a bottle

Of liquid thought in my head

Corked tight

Wouldn't want to spill it

Crash! - To the floor

Damn,

I broke it.

My mind

Pouring out

Over shattered edges

Splashing, dripping

Running away from me…

Whose idea was it to put it there anyway?

A Follower Tells Me - February 1998

Tell me all your thoughts on God

Does He really want to meet me?

A follower tells me

God's words are true

He says that He can free me

Save my soul

From eternal hell

He says that I

Should listen well

He says to keep

An open mind

And opened eyes

Great things might find

So I shall wait

To see what will be

And wonder what God

Has in store for me

Raven - February 1998

Spread your wings

And cover things

A shadow's cast

Where you have passed

The sun reflects upon your back

For you are the raven black

Your eyes are keen

And they have seen

In pantomime

The passing time

And you are the raven wise

The world is captured in your eyes

And none are greater, that is true

For none are raven, only you

My Memory - February 1998

My Memory

Falling

Fading

Growing hazy

Days of blue and gold

Age to grey and brown

Happy days

Of sun and wind

Change

To shadows and drafts

Barely breaths

Smoky bits

Clouds

Then blackness

Greyhound Bus - *February 1998*

On a Greyhound bus…

Left… Right…

Good… Evil…

God… The Devil…

My hope… My reality…

Green light… Red light…

Moving… Aren't we…?

Promise… Deception…

Light… Darkness…

So hard… So easy…

How…? Why…?

Man this is gonna be a long trip………………………………………………

On To Freedom* - *March 1998

The swords of war

Are held high

And they cry

Screams of battle

Lead them on

And keep them strong

They've broken hearts

And tattered souls

But freedom's goal

Will help them fight

Through darkest night

And bleakest day

To find their way

To reclaim

What always should be theirs

Freedom

Psychedelic* - *March 1998

P-S-Y-

C-H-E-

D-E-L-I-C

I see

Colors flashing

Thoughts crashing

Hues whirling

I'm twirling

Going crazy

Bright then hazy

What a wonder

Here I see

P-S-Y-

C-H-E-

D-E-L-I-C

The Feel - March 1998

I like the feel

Of your hands

And your breath

And your mouth

And your…

Mmm…

Yes, that

And I love the way

Your lips

Kiss my lips

Rose petal soft

And just as sweet

But just for you

And then you fill me

And enclose me

And I like it…

Mmm…

My Angel - April 1998

The world outside is cold and grey

But not so here with you

I look into your loving eyes

And I see skies of blue

The world can be unkind

And sometimes I can't help but cry

But you're there with gentle hands

To brush teardrops fallen from my eyes

We dream of sun and happiness

But times are hard all the while

Then carefully you kiss me

With warm sweet lips that make me smile

Winter's snows blanket the ground

And the wind has chilled this place

But you are here to hold me

And there's only warmth in your embrace

Yes, support and love you give me

When there are mountains we must climb

You are my strength, my heart, my angel

And I will love you 'til the end of time

Death of Love - May 1998

This is the death of love

The emptying of a soul

The quieting of sweetest whispers

The warmth thought everlasting

Has somehow gone cold

The fullness of heart

Is now utter emptiness

A sorrow so unknown

Now consumes

Such a tragedy

To have lost

Love

***Alone** - May 1998*

How alone I feel

Now that all I knew has left me

My kin have all deserted me

My pleas for love

Fell on deafened ears

I put forth forgiveness and compassion

But received contempt and silence

And how empty it leaves me

I feel guilty, hurt and angry

But I need not feel guilt

For I gave my all

And it is they who are truly empty

Devoid of soul and heart

And though the loneliness is painful

It is better this way

Pleasure & Pain - May 1998

Pleasure is an eventuality of pain…

But I close my eyes and pretend.

I am sweet and clean for them.

But why?

Why?

Because it is what the masses prefer.

My lust for anguish

To them is perversion.

To me, it's life.

When happiness is unattainable

The pain becomes necessary

And then the pain becomes joy.

I scratch my flesh

And there is pleasure in it.

I smash my skull

And I feel release,

But they don't understand.

There is no joy in blood,

No ecstasy in agony.

How small their worlds must be.

American Youth Today - May 1998

Another child lies dying

Madness reigns supreme.

Everything has gone so wrong

Right means nothing here.

I can't believe it's possible

Can any child get a gun?

America's youth are killing

No one knows what to do.

Young boys and girls have guns

Others see them as models.

Understanding nothing but rage

They kill without remorse.

Have we even got a chance

To stop this trigger madness?

Our children are killing

Death is all too common.

America's youth are becoming killers

You have to make them change.

Images Of Blue - *May 1998*

In a shade of navy blue
Are the things that I once knew
Memories of azure skies
Have faded now behind those eyes
In a hue of aquamarine
Are the times that I have seen
And in the deepest shade of cobalt
Is the place where once was my heart
In indigo oceans are crashing waves
That wash away my younger days
These shades of blue are how I live
But for other colors
My soul I would give

www.ingramcontent.com/pod-product-compliance
Ingram Content Group UK Ltd.
Pitfield, Milton Keynes, MK11 3LW, UK
UKHW051134260726
13967UKWH00010B/3041